How to Cheat in Golf

Confessions of the Handicap Committee Chairman

h. Alton Jones

54 Candles Publishing
Scottsdale, Arizona

To all the honorable golfers I have known. You know who you are – both of you.

It's good sportsmanship to not pick up lost golf balls while they are still rolling.

Mark Twain

Golf is a sport in which you yell "Fore", shoot six and write down five.

Paul Harvey

To find a man's true character, play golf with him.

P.G. Wodehouse

Table of Contents

Introduction

I recently worked as a volunteer at a tournament conducted by The American Junior Golf Association. It was a pleasure to watch as some of golf's future superstars put on a spectacular show of skill. These young men and woman are mostly of high school age, some younger, but their skill levels are indescribable. After the first day of the tournament, a kid with a 69 from the championship tees on the par 72 course didn't even finish in the top ten.

What was more spectacular than the raw talents of these young men and women was the extremely high level of professionalism, courtesy, conduct and above all else, honor. One young man, Jeffrey Miller, a high school sophomore from Phoenix, Arizona, concluded he had illegally dropped a ball during the first day of play. No one challenged him. No one knew he had done so. However, this future golf star disqualified himself from the tournament. He felt it was the right thing to do, the honorable thing to do. How many of us would have had the strength of character to do such a thing?

Fourteen year old Zach Nash was another rising golf star. In 2010, he played in the Milwaukee County Parks Tour Invitational which is put on by the Wisconsin section of the PGA. Zach won the tournament in front of his grandparents who had traveled from Iowa to see him compete. After being awarded his medal, he left the tournament venue. Later, back at his home club, he discovered he had accidentally played the tournament with a fifteenth club in his bag. It hadn't been detected. He hadn't used the club; it wasn't even his. He was home. He'd won. He held the medal. He got on the phone and called the PGA official responsible for the tournament and disqualified himself. He sent the medal back and it was awarded to the second place finisher.

These are the kinds of stories that truly bring to life the spirit of the game of golf. It is a game of honor and character. The game's essence gains breath through the honor and decency of those who play the game.

With all who enjoy fleeting glimpses of the ideal world, at some point we must return to the real world. Not all competitors share the high level of integrity displayed by these young men. Anyone who has played the game long enough to go through a sleeve of balls has probably witnessed or participated in some form of cheating. Sadly, it is common.

There are countless ways to cheat, some obvious, some not so obvious. It's happening everywhere golf is played. The more you become aware of the techniques used, you can either help put a stop to it or if your calling is from the darker side, get good at it yourself.

I remember when I was a kid, my grandfather would pull a nickel out of my ear. As a five year old boy, I was amazed – not so much that I had so many nickels in my ear, but because I knew there was trickery involved, but I couldn't quite figure out how it was done.

So it is in golf. When the same guy wins time and time again, he's just plucking nickels out of your ear and dollars out of your pocket. The goal of writing this book is to provide some hints as to where to look. If he's cheating, he can be caught.

As a mathematician, I've been able to come up with some techniques for identifying these bandits. In presenting some of these ideas in this book, I've tried to stay clear of the math as much as possible. I've made the unavoidable math as simple as I could. Unfortunately, there is a little bit of math you'll have to endure; hopefully, it will be well worth the time you spend.

After spending nearly sixty years on the golf course, I've found there are only a few ways to avoid the crooks. You can quit playing golf. You can play with the same group day-in and day-out (that's no guarantee). Or you can join'em.

After you read this book, I'll be pleased to learn you've found another way – catch'em and string'em up!

The characters in this book are purely fictional. I know they are; I've met some of them. We all have. Any resemblance between them and any real persons is only coincidental. The truth is that nearly every golf club has or has had these characters in its mix. Ages, genders and resumes may differ, but we've all met every one of the players at one time or another. Enjoy.

Acknowledgements

This book has been made possible by the selfless contribution of time and effort on the part of many people. My "review editors" invested many hours searching for and destroying my errors and typos. If any remain, they are the fault of my sister-in-law, Victoria McCarty, who is a magnificent writer in her own right. I owe a debt of gratitude to Jim Bertoni, Mike Nichols, Scott Hull and Loren Molever for offering insights and suggestions. Liz McCarty, my sweet wife of 30 years has also offered her incites and suggestions. My dear friend and golfing buddy for the past forty years, Mike Forde, put more time and effort into proofing the book than I did in writing it. But then he's a slow reader (Fresno State graduate).

To all the bandits, thieves, crooks, connivers, miscreants and cheats I have known on the golf courses around the nation, thanks for the tips. The first professional caddy I ever had was "Willie the Crook". He sent me in the right direction.

Thanks to Ron Dobkin, Jim Gabriel and Bruce Partridge for allowing me to use their images for literary and theatrical purposes.

The following terms are trademarks and service marks of the United States Golf Association: "Course Handicap™", "Equitable Stroke Control™", "ESC™", "Handicap Differential™", "Handicap Index®", "SLOPE®", "USGA®", "USGA Handicap System™".

One – Does a Golfer Cheat in the Woods?

"I told you that son of a bitch was going to win. He's the biggest sandbagger in the club."

Listen closely – somewhere in the member's grill or at the awards dinner, you'll hear that statement dripping with vinegar coming from at least one table of disgruntled losers after just about every event of  consequence. It comes with the territory. Nobody wins without becoming someone else's villain.

Is it necessarily true? Of course not. Honorable players win tournaments all the time. I saw it happen once in 1988 at Pinetop Country Club. But now that I think of it, I'm not so sure about that guy. I'm sure it's possible to win honorably; it's just hard to find examples.

At my current club (at least until this book hits the streets), one of the most honest and decent guys at our club (I know this because he told me so) won his flight in the Club Championship. He also won the

Member/Member Tournament along with its lucrative first prize money of somewhere on the order of $12,000. He also won the President's Cup and the Club Cup, a season long award with very substantial prizes and cash. He took second place in the Summer Cup, missing first by the narrowest of margins. Now that I think of it, his team has also been the winning team qualifying for a prestigious national tournament through our parent organization. It includes hotels, travel, green's fees and more. Surprisingly, he's pulled this off two years in a row despite some tough competition. Coincidentally, he is also the self-appointed president of the Men's Golf Group and a standing member of the Handicap Committee.

All this just goes to show you that it is possible for honest golfers to win tournaments. I reinforce my belief in this concept by remembering the words of my thermodynamics professor in college: "It is certainly within the realm of possibility that all of the oxygen molecules in this room will - strictly by chance - suddenly end up in one corner of this room leaving everyone not in that corner as blue, oxygen starved corpses."

It is possible. The probability can actually be calculated if you have a computer capable of managing enough digits. There is also a finite, calculable probability that one honest individual can take home half the trophies and most of the money when competing against three hundred or so other golfers, some of whom are still, after fifty years, searching for the first win of their lives.

Having been associated with a fine country club in Michigan, another one in Pinetop, Arizona and now one in Scottsdale, Arizona, I have noticed that most have the same scripts. Different actors have been cast in the roles. In some cases, the performances are better or worse, but like *Death of a Salesman*, the play is reenacted from coast-to-coast and the outcome is always the same. Some golfers are either miraculously lucky, the "perpetually serendipitous" or someone's taking some kind of liberties with handicaps. The results are the same . . . the actors are different. A high percentage of the trophyless onlookers refer to them as cheaters. Sour grapes or legitimate call?

There are countless ways to cheat in golf. Some involve the equipment and creative ways to use it. Everyone knows of the renowned "foot wedge" - traditionally used only when observing eyes are absent. Some high-stakes gamblers have been known to coat their club faces with Vaseline to reduce spin. By far and away the most common way to cheat is to massage the numbers. Handicaps were created to level the playing field, but creative cheaters have learned how to use them to their advantage. Some of the techniques are pretty obvious and easy to detect. Others are subtle, but effective. Some are nearly impossible to expose, but it can be done. There's a third kind of cheating, one that I'll call "systemic cheating". This is where the club, the tournament committee or anyone else with some control, wittingly or otherwise misapplies the rules of golf.

For most golfers, "the game" is golf. They play for the sheer enjoyment of competing in a game that cannot be mastered. For others, "the game" is "the game". And by that I mean to them it's all about gaming the system, cheating for the joy of cheating. They just can't help themselves. To those golfers, if they're not caught or at least suspected of cheating, the game loses its allure.

My grandmother used to live to play cards. One of her favorite games was cribbage, a game where points are recorded by moving pegs on a wooden board. My father didn't particularly enjoy playing cards, but when he'd visit his mother, he would always accommodate her in a game or two of cribbage.

She played to win. He played to cheat. But it was only fun if he got caught. He would intentionally move his peg a couple of extra points after each hand. He actually became quite proficient at picking up his forward peg between his thumb and forefinger and coyly picking up the back peg between his fourth finger and his pinky. He would move them simultaneously about twenty points up the board. When his mother would look down and see he was now far out in front of her, she would accuse him of cheating. He would point out that the front peg was only six points ahead of the back peg and that he had clearly only counted off six points. She would finally agree he hadn't cheated and he would laugh to the point tears would run down his face.

Every evening of cribbage ended the same way. She would magically (through his reverse cheating) come from behind and win the game. He would feign anger, stand up, curse the board, tear up the cards and throw them into the air. It was all part of the game and most of the fun. The next night, he would show up with a new deck of cards and the cheating would begin again.

Some golfers are like that. It's the cheating itself that gives them enjoyment and fulfillment. Never mind that they coincidentally seem to win more than their share of the tournaments. While you're out on the range working on your issues, they're conniving and coming up with better ways to con you out of your rightful place in the winner's circle. Some of them want to get caught or at least be suspected. Others wear metaphorical white robes and have halos that glow on the tee box. "Who me? I would never cheat."

So do golfers cheat? Hell yes they cheat. Sadly, nearly all golfers cheat, just not in the manner you might expect. Are you a cheater? Most probably yes. But the purpose of this book is to uncover the myriad ways people cheat. Only then can you decide if you want to catch them, beat them or join them.

Two – The Routine Stuff

You're not cheating if you don't know the rules.
However, at some point every golfer who competes is
going to come face-to-face with the rules of golf,
whether it's in the form of a course marshal, the club
pro, the "tournament committee" or your opponent.
Some of the more creative or compulsive among us
acquire a copy of the USGA "Rules of Golf" and we do
the unthinkable – we read the
book, all 210 pages of it. If
that's not punishment enough,
the USGA also publishes a book
entitled "Decisions on the Rules
of Golf", a seemingly endless
series of rule interpretations
made by USGA officials over
the previous couple of years. If
you still haven't satiated your
curiosity on the subject, you can
always consult (every club has

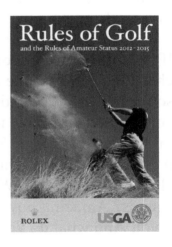

at least one), your club's self-appointed expert on the
rules. This person can quote chapter and verse on
everything from legal ball color to putter weight limits.
He's probably on the Handicap Committee and
probably recognized as "the" most boring person at the
club.

Once you have a grasp of the rules, you can now use
them to your advantage or to your opponent's

disadvantage. Everyone knows that except under a few select circumstances, the ball is to be played "as it lies". If it lands in the middle of the fairway and rolls into a deep divot, that is unfortunate, but that's where it is and that is where it should be at the time of your next stroke. But he who has the fastest cart gets there first, parks so as to block the view of the other golfers and uses the famous foot wedge to bump the ball ever so slightly out of the divot. There are a thousand and one variations on this trick and it's probably used a million times a day.

If you're above the foot wedge trick, you should at least check the ball to make sure it's not damaged. After all, someone once reported seeing a sharp stone on the course. So you follow the rules and lift the ball to inspect it for damage. Seeing none, you carefully place it precisely where it was when you lifted it – well almost where it was. What's couple of inches amongst friends? Amazing how close it came to landing in that divot. And what do you know? You caught a lucky break. The ball wasn't damaged so badly you had to replace it with a new one and it did find the only pristine patch of fairway in the area.

Some courses have hazards consisting of dry streams or washes where the vegetation can grow pretty thick. For some golfers it seems actually losing a ball in these hazards is nearly impossible. They always seem to find it. "Yes, I was playing a pink lady's ball off the tee. My wife gave it to me for my birthday." Not only that, when he found the pink ball, he had to lift it to identify it. After all, it's a two stroke penalty if you hit the wrong ball. After identifying his ball, he (of course) replaces it in the exact same spot in which he found it. Amazing how it had come to rest nicely atop the smooth, flat tuft of grass in the otherwise treacherous hazard.

Provisional balls can be handy devices for score improvement. Jack pulls his tee shot left into the trees. It may have gone through or it may be out-of-bounds. Better hit a provisional. He tees up a Titleist #3 and cuts loose. It too goes left, but not quite as far left. When he arrives in the suspect area, there sits one and only one ball. "Here's my first one – the Titleist #3," he cries. He makes a quick search for the provisional; after all, it did cost him four bucks. If he doesn't find it, he's down a

ball. If he does find it, he puts it in his pocket and is hitting his "second" shot with a brand new Titleist #3. You lose the hole.

For some golfers, cheating knows no bounds. A good friend of mine, Jim Bertoni, (above) is a golf course superintendent of some renown. He shared a story with me about a respected member of a prestigious club in Chicago. Jim was checking his course one morning when a foursome approached the green. Jim didn't want to bother the group and remained nestled in a grove of trees near the green. A member, who happened to be a Cook County Judge, hit his shot and the ball landed in a cavernous sand trap on the far side of the green. The member wasn't visible to anyone but Bertoni. Jim watched in amazement as the member took a handful of sand in one hand and his ball in the other. He threw the sand up in the air and tossed his ball greenward. "Great shot," he heard from the direction of the hole. It takes balls to play golf. It's just that some golfer's balls are bigger than others.

Another common technique is to mysteriously become arithmetically challenged at opportune moments. "What did you have there, Dave?"

"Let's see. Out-of-bounds. Had to take a drop out of the bushes. Over the green. Scuffed a chip. Onto the green. Missed the putt and then took a seven foot gimme. I had a seven." This is a particularly effective technique when you're the score keeper, especially when no one is keeping a second card.

Speaking of scorekeeping, do your best to be the scorekeeper. Here's a sure way to gain a stroke or two. "Forget" to write down the scores for a couple of holes. "Joe, what did you get on seven and eight?" Joe will be so busy trying to remember the scores he earned, chances are he's not going to remember you took a seven, not a five on the previous hole and even if he does, he's probably getting ready to tee it up and isn't going to look carefully at the card. If you do get caught, feign innocence and make the correction. You'll have other chances.

One of the most common forms of cheating involves money. I don't mean the prize money or the proceeds of your five dollar Nassau. I mean one thin dime or whatever coin or object you use to mark your ball on the green. Some golfers have developed the skills of a Las Vegas magician when it comes to ball marking. The "correct" way involves placing your mark behind the ball and then replacing the ball in the exact same spot from which you lifted it in the first place. Who controls this activity? You do and you do so with your sense of "honor". Golf is, after all, a game of "honor". On the tee box, one golfer has the "honor", but in reality, if the spirit of the game is followed, all golfers have their honor.

The problem comes when we discover that honor is severely lacking on the golf course. I could mention names here, but with the cost of printing, I can't afford to add an additional twenty pages to this book. Suffice it to say that if you watch carefully, you'll have one hell of a time not seeing it happen during every round of golf you play. The guy places his marker snugly behind his ball. When he replaces his ball, it somehow ends up an inch or so forward of the mark. The edge of the mark may or may not fall in line with the outside shadow of the ball. It may seem like a trivial advantage until you assume that with an average of two putts per hole and a gain of one to two inches per mark, you cut off about five feet of putting from the round. I hate to break it to you, but I don't make all my five footers. You've just been chiseled out of one or two strokes.

It gets better. Some golfers actually will "attempt" to place their mark where the ball actually lies. With a single, nothing-up-my-sleeve motion, the ball is retrieved as the mark is dropped. The real talented guys can actually gain an inch or so in the process. Then they'll pick up one or two more when the ball is replaced.

Another nice trick when you're the first to arrive on the green is to casually flip your mark toward the ball as you're walking toward it. If it just happens to land three or four feet in front of the ball, so be it. Close enough. Bend over and pick up your ball. The guys know that's when you're placing your mark. Pocket the ball and you've almost pocketed their money. And you still get another inch or two you can gain when you replace your ball.

If a guy uses a nice soft covered ball that gives him a lot of spin action when it lands on the green and then switches to a different ball on the putting green, he's cheating. The guy with an extra club in the bag is cheating. Gimme putts – cheating.

Some guys have been known to tee off and then move the tee blocks back a few feet. The groups that follow now have to play a course that's a little longer. Leave the green and drop a few small pebbles near the hole. "Oh my, what an unlucky break. And it was right on line." Do a lousy job of raking your trap and then leave the rake in an inappropriate spot. It's all underhanded.

This is the stuff that goes on every day on every golf course. You've got a pathetically small minority of masochists that actually play by the rules as best as they possibly can. The rest of the field wins money, tournaments and trophies. Catch'em or join'em. What's important to you? Either way, the most important thing is to know what's important to your opponent.

With these and myriad other tricks and techniques, we're talking about "point cheaters". By that I mean they're cheating at a given point in time, in a particular match. They're trying to capitalize on the moment for immediate gain. In many ways, it's the most benign form of cheating. It's the common stuff. I realize that may be like saying "It's acceptable cheating"; it's not. But it's been there since golf was invented and as long as humans are playing the game, it will be there.

The real cheating involves the "preparatory bandits" and their golfer handicaps. The overt manipulation of handicaps is the most common, yet most deceitful and insidious cheating in the game today. We'll cover that in more detail later on. It's where you can really make your money.

Three – The USGA Handicap System

The history of the USGA Handicap System dates back over 100 years. Its purpose is to allow golfers of different ability levels to compete against each other on a reasonably level playing field. Before the USGA developed its handicap system, there were undoubtedly many attempts made from the early beginnings of the game to accomplish the same thing. There are those who would argue that the consumption of 18 shots from a bottle of scotch served to make

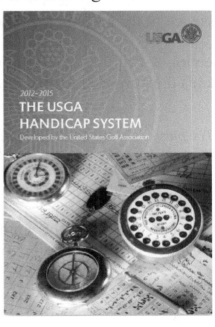

all competitors equal (and prone), but unfortunately the colorful tale about the origins of the 18 hole round and drinking a bottle of scotch have proven to be untrue. However, as an alternative to the USGA system, you might consider including in your next wager a condition that an obligatory shot of scotch be downed by the person winning each hole. I'm confident the field will soon be equalized.

The term "handicap" is said to originate from a game, "Hand in Cap", played in pubs in the 1700's. It wasn't applied to golf until the second half of the eighteenth century. There have been and continue to be many variations on the system over the years, but the entire essence of the system is to level the playing field.

Section 1-1 of the USGA Handicap System manual states the purpose of using handicaps.

> *The purpose of the USGA Handicap System is to make the game of golf more enjoyable by enabling players of differing abilities to compete on an equitable basis.*

It goes on to say that the validity of the entire system rests upon two basic assumptions.

> *Two basic premises underlie the USGA Handicap System, namely that each player will try to make the best score at every hole in every round, regardless of where the round is played, and that the player will post every acceptable round for peer review. The player and the player's Handicap Committee have joint responsibility for adhering to these premises.*

There you have it. What is the "Handicap System"? It's a system to assure fair and equitable competition. Does it work? Yes, but ONLY if everyone plays honorably and by the rules.

Do all golfers play honorably and by the rules? You bet! Sure they do. So how does the Easter Bunny color those eggs? And for that matter, does he lay the eggs himself? But I digress.

Aside from being dependent upon a golfer's honor, the entire Handicap System is also contingent upon one additional condition. Courses must be "rated" by the USGA. The USGA has reasonably well defined techniques for evaluating the playing difficulty of any given course. When rated, a course has a stroke "rating" and a "slope". The rating reflects the difficulty for a scratch golfer; the slope permits handicap adjustments for the higher handicap golfers.

For those who don't have a firm grasp of the numbers of the USGA System, here's the quick and dirty summary (with examples):

- USGA rates the course (rating 71.1, slope 129)
- Golfer wishing to play the course determines his "course handicap". USGA handicap index (17.9) times the course slope (129) divided by 113 and rounded to the closest integer. (17.9 x 129 / 113 = 20.4 which rounds to 20)

- Golfer plays the course with 20 handicap and shoots 92.
- Golfer posts 92 (neglecting "equitable stroke control" – read the manual) and also posts the course rating and slope for the tees played. The difference between the score and the course rating is the differential that's used to calculate his next handicap index. (92 − 71.1 = 20.9)
- At the next handicap revision date, the best ten of the golfer's previous twenty scores (differentials) are averaged. That number is multiplied by 96% and rounded to one decimal place. That is the golfer's new handicap index.

It's interesting to note that the USGA says a handicap index is a measure of a golfer's "potential ability". I've got the potential to score an eagle on every hole on the golf course. The odds of that happening in one round are much worse than the ability of most calculators to display the number. However, I do have that potential. So when our local rules Nazi ran through the club professing to be an expert on all things USGA, members had to incessantly listen to "It's a measure of a golfer's potential." Clearly the USGA's definition of "potential" and my definition weren't in complete alignment. I looked harder for their definition and finally found it.

In a nutshell, a player's "potential ability" is measured by the Handicap Index as calculated using the methods set forth by the USGA. In other words, the Handicap Index is a measure of the "potential" which is defined by the Handicap Index. For those of you into circular arguments, I'm confident this makes perfect sense. It's sort of like spending hours trying to solve a complex mathematical equation and finally working it down and proving that one equals one.

Rather than quibble over definitions, let's take a step back and ask the question, "Does the USGA Handicap System serve to level the playing field and promote fair and equitable competition?" After reviewing tens of thousands of rounds of golf, I'm confident it does an excellent job. However, it is completely dependent upon having fair courses, i.e., courses rated accurately by the USGA, and knowledgeable and honest golfers. In the ideal world, it's all fair. It's so unfortunate that so few tournaments are played in the ideal world.

Four - The Biggest Cheat in Golf

Unless you're a tour player or at least a better than scratch golfer or you're playing with the same equally matched golfers every game, your competitive golf is played with handicaps applied to your round. According to the USGA, handicaps are intended to level the playing field, to give everyone an equal chance at winning. As a mathematician and a

Handicap Committee chair, I've spent more than a small amount of time double-checking the math of the USGA. Frankly, the USGA Handicap System does a very good job of accomplishing the goal, especially when properly applied and used. Therein lays the problem. It is rarely "properly applied".

As often as not, mistakes are made from a lack of knowledge of the system. A misunderstanding of "equitable stroke control", scores posted when they shouldn't be or scores not posted when they should be result in handicaps that are incorrect. The level playing field is no longer level.

Perhaps the greatest contributor to handicap inaccuracies is a lack of knowledge as to how to actually keep score. How many times have you heard someone say, "Just give me a double-bogey"? This after hitting a tee shot out-of-bounds, rolling the second tee shot down the fairway, chunking a five-iron to within fifty yards of the green, sculling the next shot into the bunker, taking three to get out and missing the next two putts. Surely that's fair; after all, the hole was lost to the competitor. What's the difference if you write down a six or an eleven?

Well the difference is, you're going to post the score. Your handicap is going to reflect that five stroke difference. You're going to end up with a lower handicap than you have truly earned. You're then going to compete in the Club Championship against other guys that have honest handicaps. You're screwed. You don't stand a chance.

Admittedly, if you're a single digit handicapper, you can post no worse than a six on a par four hole, but golfers with handicaps up to nineteen can post sevens. Those from twenty to twenty-nine can post eights. If they take one six per round when an eight or higher is in order, they've lowered their handicaps by two strokes! If you're going to play in tournaments, what the hell do you expect when you spot the field two strokes?

You have cheated. The only problem is you've cheated yourself. When you sit back and notice the same guys end up on top of the leaderboard in most of your tournaments, you shouldn't be terribly surprised. They may not be the cheaters. YOU may be the cheater.

"Ego handicaps" are as common as missed putts. When I was in my thirties, I routinely carried a mid-single digit handicap. Now that a few extra decades have wandered past, I'm up into the double-digit range. Would I like to be single digit again? Well, of course I would. But I'm not. And I'm not going to be. Is it hard to accept? It used to be, but of the many lessons that can be gleaned from golf, I've had to accept and am now finally comfortable with the fact that I'm no longer thirty. I can live with it, especially, given my knowledge that in most tournaments, I'm going to beat the hell out of those guys whose egos haven't let them come to grips with reality yet. If that's you, you're spotting me a couple of strokes. Thanks.

Ego and oblivion are two paths to the same destination. Some people can't deal with the diminished ego. Others end up with the equivalent of an ego handicap simply because they're oblivious to the problems they cause themselves.

Consider these guys; you know them all. You may be one of them. Your competitor finds his drive in the rough, buried. It's deep enough that he's got to leave

his hat by the ball to keep from losing it while he goes
to get his club. No one's around. A wee little bump of
the ball improves his lie enough so he doesn't break his
arm trying to hit it from its dungeon. It probably saved
him a stroke, maybe two. And there is a dollar Nassau
on the line. As an old acquaintance told me, "Anything
worth having is worth cheating to get." He justifies his
actions by thinking you'd probably do the same thing
and he's just leveling the playing field. The problem
now is that if he does this once per round then his
handicap is roughly one stroke lower than it should be.
What if he does it three times per round? The last thing
in the world you want is to get stuck with this turkey as
a partner in the Member/Member tournament.

Gimme putts cost you tournaments. Show me someone
that hasn't missed a sixteen inch putt and I'll show you
someone that has never played golf. We call them
"sweepers". "Within the leather" or "within view of the
hole", some guys pick'em up and count them as one-
putts. If you're picking them up without putting them
into the hole, you're cheating. You're cheating yourself.
Your handicap is artificially low. Your chances of
winning the big events are miniscule.

Here's another common contributor to the ego
handicap. You're engaged in a match play competition.
You lie four on the green twenty-five feet from the
hole. Your opponent's ball is just outside your ball, but
he lies two. He runs his putt a couple inches from the

hole and taps in for par. You've lost the hole and he concedes your putt. What score do you write down? If you said, "five", you're wrong. The USGA Handicap manual says that if the hole is not completed, you write down your "most probable" score. The odds of you making a twenty-five foot putt are pretty low. There's a good chance you'll two-putt. You write down a six. Otherwise, you've cheated yourself again.

How many golfers declare "ground under repair" in opposition to the green keeper? "Well, it should have been ground under repair. I'm taking a drop." Dew on the fairway is not "casual water". An ant is not a "burrowing animal". Moving "loose impediments" does not include recontouring the landscape. In the game of golf, you play the ball where it lies. Any time you improve your lie, you're cheating. You're cheating yourself.

It is not uncommon to see golfers playing the game with handicaps that are a full five or six strokes below what their legitimate handicaps should be. You won't see them at the trophy presentation unless you're looking to the back of the room where they're sitting with their buddies bitching about another loss and how that same S.O.B. has won again. Yes. There's a good chance that the biggest cheater at your golf club is you. And you're cheating no one other than yourself.

Five – Managing the Numbers

With the ego handicappers putting themselves at such a disadvantage, it almost seems unnecessary to cheat to win. But if you're going to win consistently, you've got to somehow get an edge on those other crumbs that are smart enough to write the correct scores on their cards, play their balls down and putt out on every hole. These are the guys that stand a chance of winning. Not that their golf games are that much better. Their preparation is better.

By "preparation", I don't mean pounding balls on the driving range or getting that "tune-up" lesson from the club pro; I mean managing the numbers.

The entire essence of the USGA Handicap System rides on a couple of assumptions. One is that you will honestly try to get your best score on every hole you play. The other is that you will properly post every round of golf you play, but ONLY if it is a "postable" round. Good number managers are intimately familiar with these assumptions and they work them to the fullest. More importantly, they know how to work them in subtle, non-obvious ways.

The USGA Handicap System manual defines postable versus non-postable rounds. In truth, common sense tells us which rounds should and shouldn't be posted. If you go out and play a round with three clubs rather than the fourteen allowed, the round is not a postable round. If you play a round with eighteen clubs, don't post that round. Play two balls – don't post. If you're out playing couples golf and trying to impress the ladies with your trick shots, you're not trying to get your best score on every hole. Don't post. A "fun" round where you tee off while standing on an inner-tube and you putt with a broom is not a postable round.

A good numbers manager knows that everyone makes a mistake from time to time. Try as he might, every once in a while amidst the hustle and bustle of a golfer's life, he might forget to post a round, especially if it's six strokes below his handicap. At the same time, a cluttered memory might cause one to forget he has already posted a round and he might accidentally post it twice, especially if it's six strokes over his handicap. "Ah, but you can't do that," you say. "When posting over the internet, the computer will tell you it's a double posting." Not if you forget to change the date when you post it on the day following the round.

Another popular trick is to post by manually writing your score on the posting sheet at the club and then posting again the following day on-line. This is one of the reasons more and more clubs are no longer using the old fashioned, hand-written posting sheets.

"Equitable Stroke Control" is another great tool for number manipulation. Most golfers who have played long enough to get a handicap should know about equitable stroke control. The USGA's statisticians have implemented ESC to help keep the "manipulators" from racking up sixteen pars, a birdie and a four-putt twelve on the last hole to elevate their handicaps. In their defense, some guys truly don't know or remember what their maximum scores per ESC are for posting purposes. But they understand that the rules exist and they fully grasp the concept. "What did I shoot, Joe? I've got to post my score", says Bob.

"I've got you for an 85," Joe replies. Joe overlooks the fact that the 85 included an eight on the par three fifth hole. Bob has a nine handicap and can post no more than a double-bogey. He should be posting an 82, not an 85. Oh well, mistakes happen. Bob wins the next club tournament by a stroke. He's now a ten.

Even if Joe said, "I've got you for an 85, but your adjusted score is 82," there's a good chance that by the time Bob gets to the posting computer, he'll forget to adjust. Maybe he just didn't hear Joe. Maybe he also kept his own card and knows damn good and well what to post, but the club championship is coming up in three weeks.

It's amazing how a group of highly educated people become arithmetically challenged when holding a golf scorecard and a pencil. After reviewing thousands of scorecards, I have found that more than ten percent of them have errors in simple addition. You would expect the task of summing eighteen (usually) single-digit numbers wouldn't be daunting, but apparently it's more difficult than you might imagine. A truly devious scorekeeper could easily deduct a stroke from a competitor's score while inadvertently adding it to his own. One handicap trends downward while another trends up. In handicap management, the little things add up – just not always correctly.

Another miraculous alignment of the stars seems to occur on the first and sixteenth days of the month. Were you aware that statistically speaking, golfers play better on the first and the sixteenth? I'm sure it's just a coincidence that this happens even though the observation is based upon more than 100,000 holes of golf in my database. To suggest otherwise would be to say someone is engaged in handicap manipulation. However, if manipulation were involved (golfer's don't cheat, do they?), it could be explained by realizing that in the United States, handicap revisions occur after the end of the day on the last day of the month and the fifteenth day of the month. If a golfer fires a round on the last day of the month that was six strokes above his handicap and he knows that round will knock out one that was six below his handicap, he will swim across a flaming pond of gasoline to make absolutely sure that round gets posted before the revision takes place. On the other hand, if he shoots a 75 that will lower his handicap by a full stroke, he will undoubtedly do his absolute best to make sure that score is posted within the next day or so. The club championship is coming up soon so he has a lot on his mind, but he'll definitely try to remember.

In theory, your club's handicap committee is keeping a close eye on all these matters. But after serving on a handicap committee, I can assure you there's greater gain in believing in Santa Claus than believing in the handicap committee. More on this later.

The USGA encourages "peer review". There is absolutely no reason you shouldn't be double-checking your competitor's scores. There are many ways to do this and you'll be doing not only yourself a favor, but you'll be helping out your competitor, "poor Bob". After all, you know Bob wants to do what's right, especially before the club championship.

Another common refrain is "our handicaps don't travel well." It shouldn't come as a big surprise to anyone that if you're playing the same course three times per week, you tend to become familiar with the roll of the greens, the shortcuts, the tricks, the dangers and the other nuances of your course that allow you to score well. When you play a new course, one you've never stepped on before, you're usually at a bit of a disadvantage. You don't know the greens, the dangers, the places where the ball rolls toward the water. On average, golfers score higher relative to their handicaps when they're playing "away" courses.

The matter of handicaps not "traveling well" is another issue worthy of consideration. At any golf course, the club pro and the golf course superintendent – if given enough truth serum – will admit that it sometimes seems the biggest part of their jobs is to listen to the incessant bitching of a crotchety herd of retired bastards that are frantically clinging to the memories of their past power. "The rough is too deep." The tee boxes aren't level." "Pin placements suck." "Those damn guys on the mowers are interfering with my putting." Like the tide, the whining goes on without quarter. It becomes almost irresistible for the staff to set the course up to mitigate some of the complaining. The end result is that courses tend to play a little easier than their USGA ratings. Member's scores tend to be a little lower. Their handicaps then tend to be a little lower. Now they play an away course where the course is set up as it was when it was rated and scores balloon. The handicaps don't "travel well".

We're now looking at another great way to manipulate a handicap. You can do so with complete honor and with complete honesty by simply playing other courses, ones that tend to setup according to their USGA rating. Your scores will tend to be higher, even after you become familiar with the courses. Your handicap will grow and you'll have a very substantial advantage over those at your club that restrict their play to their home course. You've done absolutely nothing wrong other than capitalize on your home course pro's fatigue from fighting the irresistible force, i.e., the bitchers.

Let's take this one step further. Let's look at the "away" play in the shadows, the darker side. Here's where tournaments can really be won. Your handicap is built on your honor. The problem is – not everyone has the same amount of honor. If you're playing alone and you shoot a round at your handicap, but post the round as five strokes above your handicap, who's going to know? If you're playing on your home course, there's a pretty good chance someone else will know. Too many eyes lurking in the rough to get away with grand theft.

But if you're playing an away course and you get paired up with total strangers or bring a fellow crook with you, the strangers probably won't remember your name the next morning, let alone your score or your home club. Furthermore, they won't give a tinker's damn if you posted, posted correctly or threw your clubs in the pond. Knock yourself out Capone! Post whatever you want. What the hell do you think the Handicap Committee's going to do – subpoena your scorecard? Eat it quickly when you hear the knock of the process server on your door.

So if the odds of getting busted by posting erroneous scores at away clubs are fairly low, why don't some golfers do that? They do! It's far more common than you might think. Can you catch them? Unless they understand the laws of statistics better than you do, you bet you can catch them.

The USGA Handicap System is soundly based upon the laws of statistics. Without going into the intimate details, I'll try and give you a glimpse of some of inviolate laws that are in play here and how they can be used to catch a crook.

Here's where it may get a little dry, but you need to take the medicine if you're going to cure the ailment. We're concerned with two basic and related statistical "distributions". To simplify the topic, I'm going to assume a player is an experienced golfer, has an established handicap, and routinely plays the same course under the same conditions and that there are no significant outside influences on his game, e.g., injuries, golf lessons, etc. With that said, every golfer has an "average eighteen hole score". It is related to, but definitely not the same as his handicap. Also every golfer has an "average to par per hole". An eighteen handicap golfer for example will tend to have an average "per hole" score of [cue the music]... a bogey. So far, no big revelations.

In both cases, there will be a distribution around the average or mean. The eighteen handicapper may shoot 90, 86, 89, 93, 95 and an 87 in six consecutive rounds and average 90. However, the odds are overwhelming he's not going to shoot six straight 90s. The same argument applies to the "per hole" score. If he's going to average 90, he's going to average one over par on each hole. But it will be rare when he scores eighteen straight bogeys.

In each case, the distribution of scores around the mean is frequently approximated with a standard bell curve. (In reality, the curve is more of a gamma-distribution, but I promised to try and keep things simple and a bell curve is close enough for everything we're going to do here.)

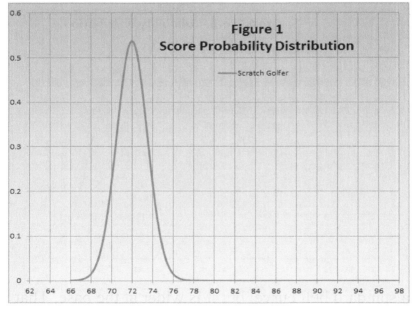

Figure 1 shows the distribution of scores for a typical scratch golfer. The peak of the curve falls at about 72;

that's close to the average score for a scratch golfer on a course with a USGA rating of 69.0. Statistically, a scratch golfer's standard deviation runs at a little over two strokes. What that means is that approximately seventy percent of his scores will fall between 70 and 74, i.e., one standard deviation from the mean. Roughly ninety-five percent of his scores will be within two standard deviations of the mean, i.e., between 68 and 76.

Figure 2 presents the same information for a bogey golfer. Notice that the curve remains an approximation

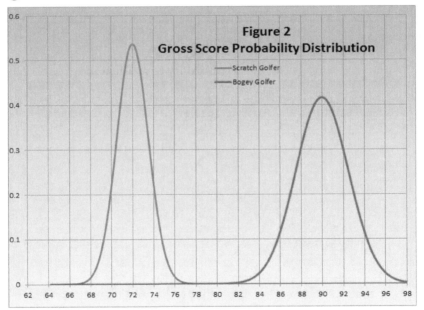

to a standard bell curve, but it is wider at the base. That says a bogey golfer's standard deviation tends to be higher than that of a scratch golfer, somewhere on the order of four strokes. The bogey golfer's scores will average approximately 90 with about seventy percent of them falling within one standard deviation of the mean, i.e., between 86 and 94 and about ninety-five percent falling within two standard deviations between 82 and 98. The range of scores is greater for a bogey golfer than a scratch golfer. This is why you see the higher handicap golfers at your club more commonly associated with those dreaded net 61s while the scratch guys generally can't get close to net scores that low (without being arrested for larceny).

A couple of comments are in order relative to the previous paragraphs. I'm taking some liberties by using averages as if they were USGA Handicaps. I've done this for the sole purpose of keeping the discussion simple. All of the same arguments apply, but with some slight mathematical complications. Handicaps are based upon ninety-six percent of the best ten score differentials of the last twenty rounds. I see no need to complicate the math here when the qualitative results are the same. Given the details of the USGA formulas, the average net score of a golfer is approximately three strokes over the course rating. The standard deviation for a scratch golfer is slightly higher than two strokes and increases with increasing handicap.

With this basic statistical understanding, let's now catch a thief. Joe is one of those guys that is habitually serendipitous. He seems to win substantially more than his share of the events at the club. He also plays a larger than average number of rounds away from his home club or knows how to find those courses on the GHIN posting website. He sports an eighteen handicap, but when playing in tournaments, he seems to shoot net 65 or so with a fair amount of regularity. He claims he's just a good tournament player and has the ability to "focus" a little better than most when the pressure's on.

As an eighteen, his average score should be roughly three strokes plus his handicap above the course rating. If the home course is rated 69.0, he should be averaging approximately 90 strokes per round at home. You go into the USGA's GHIN system and get a record of his

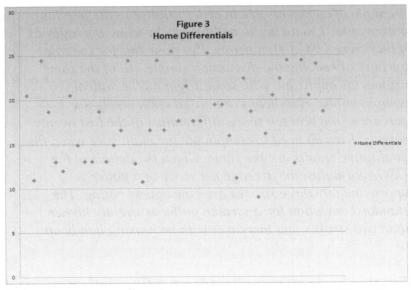

scores. (You can do this yourself or ask your Handicap Committee or pro-shop to do it for you.) Figure 3 shows a plot of his home scores. After you average his home scores, you find he averages about 86 strokes per round. Something doesn't seem to be right and there's a strange odor emanating from the data. "Well, I play a lot at other courses and our handicaps just don't travel well so I shoot higher." A common refrain, but let's look closer.

With a hand calculator and a basic understanding of statistics, you determine his average home score is 86.1 with a standard deviation of 4.6 strokes. These numbers are reasonable and consistent – for a golfer with a fourteen handicap. Obviously, the away scores are the ones that have brought his handicap up to an eighteen. Is that possible? Sure. Among the other possible explanations, maybe, his course handicap doesn't travel well. But the truth is the odor is starting to become more of a stench. Shall we look closer yet?

Figure 4 shows the scores over time for a golfer who shall remain unnamed. When you look at his home scores [diamonds on the chart], the distribution is perfectly normal, i.e., the number of scores over and under the average are reasonable and magnitude of the deviations from the average are as you would expect for a golfer in his handicap range. Roughly seventy-percent fall within the range of 86 to 94. However, when you look at away scores over the same time period [squares on the chart], a couple of very odd things appear.

The first is that the average score is about five strokes higher than the home score average. This is not out of the question if our guy is playing a large number of "different" away courses. Maybe the handicap really doesn't travel well. Unfamiliarity with the away courses

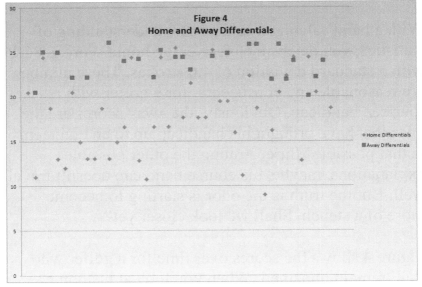

can result in higher scores. But after playing the same course a dozen times, it is no longer an unfamiliar course. The scores should begin to line up with your home course scores. In this case, they clearly do not. Shall we get the air-freshener?

What really sticks out, however, is the grouping of the away scores. Statistically speaking, the standard deviation of the away scores should be a little higher than for the home scores or at least no lower. In this case, the standard deviation has fallen from 4.6 for the home scores to 1.7 for the away scores. Is that reasonably possible? Sure, just like it is possible that all of the oxygen molecules in the room coincidentally migrate to one corner of the room at the same instant in time. It's possible, just not very probable. Oh bullshit! It's not possible. The only reasonable explanation is that our guy gets writer's cramp when posting away scores or that after selecting "away" from the GHIN system's posting screen, certain number keys on his keyboard mysteriously become disabled. Look at the away postings on the chart. It's as if the entire lower half of the normal distribution is missing. What do you say to this guy? Try, "You have a right to remain silent. Anything you say can and will be used against you."

Six – Strategies for Team Games

Most golfers enjoy playing team games. They come in all sizes and colors. Best ball out of two, best two out of four, one ball on six holes, two on the next six, three for five and all four balls count on the last hole. In the *Jones Golf Management* software program, there are well over one hundred different game formats that can be selected at the touch of a button. More are added as the need arises.

When playing team games, there's some relief in knowing your triple-bogey didn't count against your team's score. Who isn't relieved after surviving the suspense and drama of having all four balls count and watching his twenty foot putt drop in the hole for victory? At the same time, who isn't relieved after three putting from six feet when he discovers his ball isn't needed for the team score? Team games can be fun and interesting diversions.

Unfortunately, even if every golfer in the field is a saintly adherent of the spirit of the USGA handicap system (the last documented instance of this occurred in 1903 at a club with only three holes in Canal Winchester, Ohio), there are simply no handicapped team games where some balls don't count that are inherently fair and equitable.

Before we address the problems with team games, let's talk about the third type of cheating in golf – "systemic cheating". There are fundamentally three ways of cheating in golf. We've already talked about two of them. The first is the obvious, taking steps during a competitive round to gain an unfair advantage. We've considered the foot-wedge, improper ball marking and the like. The second type of cheating I'll call "preparatory cheating". That's when the handicap numbers are manipulated before a game is played. This is what is normally referred to as sandbagging. I'll call the third type of cheating "systemic cheating". This is where the competition format and/or the makeup of the teams in the competition are manipulated to the advantage of one group and the disadvantage of another.

Team play opens the door for both the "preparatory cheats" and the "systemic cheats". We've already discussed sandbaggers and I'll have more to say later. But what about the "systemic cheats"?

In many of the cases, those responsible for the unfair formats aren't even aware they're setting them up. Sadly, some tournament committees are headed up by individuals that are so arithmetically challenged that discussions of the math associated with anything other than the simplest format prompts catatonic stares into the oblivion of outer-space. Talk of how the USGA Handicap System works or why handicap allowances are recommended for certain game formats is so far above their pay-grade that you begin to understand how the original Navajo Code Talkers must have felt when no one outside of Chinle, Arizona understood a word they were saying.

Here are a couple of real world examples. Were they deceitfully malicious or were they the products of benign ignorance? I can only guess, but either way, the results were the same. Team games were set up where a portion of the field had a distinct advantage over the rest of the field.

In the first case, Willie, a personal friend of Bud, the head of the member/member tournament committee has long had a propensity for incessant complaining about any injustice, real or imagined, that would put him at a disadvantage in competition. Any injustice that gave him a favorable position always lay muffled in a thick blanket of silence. When an attempt was made to play fairly, the whining would begin. "I'm not going to play in anymore tournaments," he'd tell his pal Bud. "It's unfair to us older guys. We don't hit the ball as far as we used to; we should be allowed to play from the forward tees," Willie'd whine.

Well, the guy with the big hat, Bud, wanted to please his pals so he kicked around the idea and decided he would declare, "If your age plus your handicap equals ninety or more, you can play in the club's major tournaments from the forward tees." Some of the other members began complaining and Bud decreed, "Well of course we'll adjust handicaps appropriately for the change in tee box assignments."

This was all fine and dandy, but for reasons that remain a mystery, the handicaps were not correctly adjusted. Many clubs have similar rules to encourage their more senior members to participate in club events. The techniques to be used to adjust handicaps when playing from different tees in a competition are very clearly specified with detailed examples in the USGA Handicap manual. (Handicaps must be adjusted to reflect the difference in the course slope and then adjusted for the difference in course rating when comparing the two tee boxes in question.) In this case, the difference in course rating was not taken into account.

What this amounted to was that the players that could tee off from the forward tees were being given two extra shots in every round. The Member/Member Tournament was, with the exception of the Club Championship, the biggest tournament of the year. It was played over forty-five holes. The quid-pro-quo was that the Willie the whiner would stop his complaining and in exchange, Bud, the tournament committee head would spot him five strokes in the tournament. Now, never mind that with the calcutta the night before the tournament began, prize money was well into five-digit country, it still boiled down to waiving a fundamental rule of golf – either out of ignorance or to benefit a buddy.

Taken directly from The USGA Handicap System manual:

Q: May golf clubs' choose not to follow Section 3-5 of "The USGA Handicap System" manual if the club's groups are competing from different tees?

A: No, ignoring Section 3-5 of The "USGA Handicap System" when players are competing from different tees would be waiving a Rule of Golf. The Committee in charge of a competition does not have the authority to waive a Rule of Golf.

When a newly appointed member of the Handicap Committee challenged the decision to not implement the rule correctly, the big wig turned a deaf ear. Our club's "I know the rules" guy, Humphrey, didn't pick up on the problem; he knew something wasn't right, but suggested that Willie, the chief whiner in this drama, wasn't on the up-and-up and that the Handicap Committee should adjust his and only his handicap. "He hasn't established a handicap from the white tees," said the "expert". He didn't seem to grasp the fact that a handicap index isn't dependent upon which tees are played. The other forward tee players could escape with their five gift strokes. The club pro was new to the job and between the rule book and the politics, was buried in conflict. It was taken directly to the club general manager (a private corporation actually owns the club). A golf professional himself, he listened to an explanation of the dilemma. For reasons one can only guess, the tournament was played in clear violation of the rules and tens of thousands of dollars were distributed to the winners while the losers sat in befuddled amazement trying to understand what happened.

That is a classic example of "systemic cheating". Was it cheating or was it ignorance? Does intent define the crime? If I'm one of the guys that fell one stroke out of the money to someone who was improperly given a five stroke spot, I'm going to feel like I was cheated.

Another classic example of "systemic cheating" has gone on for years at many clubs. This one's a little less clear, but in the final analysis, it's cheating nonetheless. The USGA "recommends" the use of "handicap allowances". The head of the tournament committee has steadfastly refused to adopt the USGA's recommendation. It's not clear if Bud doesn't understand the reasoning behind it or if he simply doesn't want the playing field leveled in accordance with the spirit of the USGA Handicap System itself, maybe both. Admittedly, he's been pressured incessantly by Willie and the other resident whiners who complain about their handicaps being lowered for a tournament. Forget that everyone else also has his handicap lowered by the same percentage. "It's just not fair. I'm not playing in any more tournaments if that's the way you're going to be!" Bud, the committee head and Humphrey, his "I know all the rules" guy, justify the actions by saying, "They are only USGA recommendations. That means we don't have to accept them. If they were important, they'd be rules rather than recommendations."

Without belaboring the statistics, let me explain the USGA's recommendations and tell you why I believe they're only "recommendations" and not "requirements". The USGA says that in certain team games, e.g., one best ball out of two, handicaps should be reduced by a certain percentage. They go on to say that under certain circumstances, there should be limitations on the spread between handicaps on any team. For example, a two man team with a two handicap golfer paired with a thirty-two handicap golfer is not recommended. I'll use the "four-ball", i.e., the one best net ball out of the two man team as my example below. In this case, the USGA recommends all handicaps be reduced to ninety-percent of the values for the tournament play. This is all explained thoroughly in Section 9.4 of the USGA Handicap System manual.

To understand why handicap allowances are necessary, we return to the bell curve. When looking at the probability distributions of scores for a scratch golfer and for a bogey golfer (Figure 6), remember the scratch golfer will average approximately par on every hole. The highest point on the curve (view as the highest probability) is at roughly par. The odds of scoring one stroke over or under par are less, but not far from equal. Two strokes above or below par certainly show up on

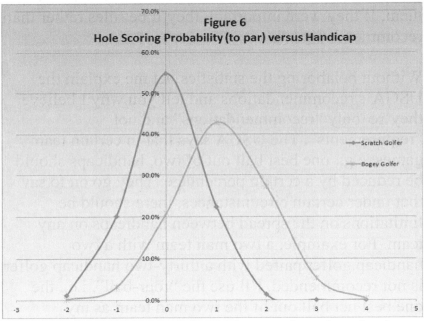

Figure 6
Hole Scoring Probability (to par) versus Handicap

the scratch golfer's card from time to time, but that's about where it ends. Gross double-eagles (albatross) are extremely rare.

The probability curve for the bogey golfer has its peak at approximately a bogey. That's precisely what you would expect. The odds of scoring one below or one above bogey are, like the scratch golfer, lower, but still significant. But here's where the curves become different. Two strokes below the average for the scratch golfer is a very low number. Not so for the bogey golfer. Bogey golfers get their share of natural birdies, not as many as scratch golfers, but as blind hogs and turnips suggest, bogey golfers occasionally slap one up close to the hole on the three pars. Hence the odds of a bogey golfer scoring two strokes below his average score are significantly higher than the odds of a scratch golfer scoring two strokes below his average. The same can be said for higher scores. Bogey golfers will tend to have many more holes two strokes above their average than a scratch golfer.

It all makes complete sense. On a gross basis, the scratch golfer is going to slaughter the bogey golfer almost every time. The question becomes, "How can the scratch golfer and the bogey golfer go out and play a round head-to-head and have any chance of the game being competitive or even fair?"

Hey! Here's an idea. Let's come up with a system where the average scores are totaled. We throw a little butter and mustard on the spread by taking the best ten out of the last twenty and then just for the hell of it, we'll take ninety-six percent of that number. We'll adjust it further for difficulty for the bogey golfers versus the scratch golfers and call that a slope adjustment. We'll round it off. Then the difference between those two numbers will be deducted from the higher scoring player. Everything's equal. The playing field is level. We have an interesting and competitive match. I'll call it a "handicap system". Great idea! Damn, I'm a genius. Hang on – someone's saying something in my headset.

I've just been told that someone has stolen my idea. And they did it over a hundred years ago. Wait . . . there's more. The USGA has adopted that system and they . . . what? . . . they've named it the "Handicap System". Those thieving bastards!

Alright – fine. I'm writing a book and don't have time to quibble over trifles. I'll let my attorneys work out the details later. In the meantime – for the purposes of this

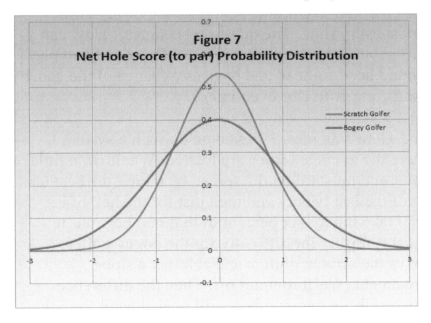

Figure 7
Net Hole Score (to par) Probability Distribution

discussion – Figure 7 shows what happens when the handicap is applied and the score probability curves suddenly refer to "net" scores rather than gross scores. The highest probability for both the scratch and bogey golfers falls at net par. Game on! Field level. Fair match. And fun was had by all.

Bob Ritz, a good friend of mine who was on the ground floor of a little company called Tommy Bahama, told me about how he played a twenty-five cent Nassau for an entire golf season against his friend, Jim Boaz. After about fifty rounds, Jim owed Bob seventy-five cents. Funny how handicaps leveled the playing field there. (Twenty-five cent Nassau? And I thought Tommy Bahama was supposed to be a big company!)

Meanwhile, onward toward the injustice of team games (and you thought I forgot). As you look at Figure 7, it's clear the bogey golfer's net scores average the same as the scratch golfer's scores. The bogey golfer scores a few more net birdies and eagles than the scratch golfer, but he also fumbles his way into a few more net double-bogeys and triple bogeys. It's pretty much all square when the stick is put back into the 18th hole.

I'll try to resist the almost insatiable urge to throw myself into the actual statistical calculations; just trust me on this (or drop me an email and I'll be delighted to swap numbers with you – my favorite equation (next to the Schrödinger) is a third-order Bessel function). But look closely at Figure 7. When adjusted for net scores, the bogey golfer stands a much greater chance of scoring a net birdie or net eagle than does the scratch golfer. The bogey golfer is more inconsistent and the width of the base of his probability curve is wider. (Remember the standard deviation as a function of a player's handicap increases with increasing handicap.)

My hands are shaking with the desire to go quantitative into statistics at this point, but I'm just going to suck it up. Here's the truism. In a game where two man teams count only their one best ball, two scratch golfers going up against a scratch golfer and a bogey golfer are screwed!

For illustrative purposes, assume the scratch golfer's odds of getting a net and gross (he's getting no strokes) birdie or better are one-in-five. (The actual probability is approximately 0.787.) Conversely, he'll score gross par or higher four out of five, i.e., 80% of the time. Assume the odds of a bogey golfer getting a gross par (net birdie) or better are one-in-four. (The actual probability is approximately 0.758.) Hence the chances a bogey golfer will score a gross bogey (net par) or higher are three out of four or about 75% of the time. The probability that both players on a two-man team shoot above net birdie can be estimated by multiplying the probabilities of the individual golfers shooting net par or above.

That means the odds the team of two scratch golfers scoring net par or higher are approximately (0.8 x 0.8) or 64%. The chances of the scratch and bogey golfer scoring net par or higher are (0.75 x 0.8) or about 60% of the time. By subtracting those numbers from 100%, we can conclude the scratch/scratch golfer combo will shoot net birdie 36% of the time while the scratch golfer paired with the 18 handicapper will score net birdie 40% of the time. Pair two 18 handicappers together and the odds of one or the other shooting net birdie increase to 44%; the edge grows. Clearly, one team has an advantage over the other.

"Well, sure," you say, "the odds of the bogey golfer shooting double-bogey are higher."

You bet, Bubba. The only problem is that that ball doesn't count. Point, set, match to the bogey guys.

For those of you with a mathematical background, it will be apparent I've taken some minor liberties with the numbers. But I've done so only in the interest of keeping the explanation simple. Although there may be slight quantitative differences if we sharpen the pencil a bit, qualitatively, we're right on the money. The combination of the bogey golfer and the scratch golfer carries and uses a big can of "whoop-ass" when they play against the low handicappers. Is it possible that the two scratch guys can beat the loaded team? Sure.

Remember the oxygen molecules. But the deck is stacked against them.

We came up with a novel idea to level the playing field when individuals compete. (I'm still annoyed the USGA stole my idea over a hundred years back). Surely we can do the same in the case of team play. My idea here is to equip every golf cart with a personal computer and that the official scorekeeper has an assistant assigned for every round of golf played. Just like the pilot has his navigator, the scorekeeper will have his statistical navigator who runs the computer program that assigns fractional strokes on every hole or even every swing. The statistical navigator must have a minimum of at least a bachelor's degree in mathematics from a major institution of higher learning such as Michigan State University or the University of Arizona – maybe even Fresno State.

Hold tight. I'm getting some more comments in my headset. "Same to you fella!" The guys don't seem to agree with me on my idea. In fact, they're suggesting I get some counseling. I assume they mean golf lessons. I am having a little trouble with a hook right now.

Alright, let's see what the USGA says we do here. It appears they are "recommending" we use "handicap allowances" in certain situations. I'll leave the details to you and the USGA Handicap System manual, but in the case of a one best ball out of two situation, they recommend ninety percent of the player's handicaps be used. One best ball out of four? They recommend eighty percent of handicaps be used. They take it a step further and suggest that the difference between the high and low handicap players be limited to a maximum amount. Pair a scratch golfer with a thirty handicapper and the high handicapper will be adjusted way down.

Note that these are not the "rules". They are only "recommendations". As the Handicap Committee chair at one club, I listened to the mathematically unenlightened leaders of the tournament committee as they argued against the use of handicap allowances. "They're only recommendations," Bud proclaimed. "If they truly thought they should be used all the time, they would have made them rules." I hung my head in amazement and wondered why the hell I ever agreed to be on the Committee.

So why are they only recommendations? I'm confident they are only recommendations because they are not mathematically rigorous solutions to the problems. They are only approximations. After reviewing the statistics of a few million holes of golf played, the USGA has concluded they are pretty good approximations, so in the interest of providing a simple, easily applied solution to the problem, they have recommended handicap allowances. If they were to insist on their use in the form of a hard rule, someone could easily challenge them and argue that a ninety percent allowance does not have the exact same effect on teams where handicaps are spread by five strokes as it does on teams with spreads of ten strokes. For those of us who truly want a more defensible solution to the dilemma, we can return to my idea of cart computers and math majors on every team. But I will confess that worrying about someone getting 1.041 strokes on a hole rather than 1.0 stroke is perhaps a bit of overkill. I'll go along with the ninety percent allowance.

As an entertaining aside, I'll mention the reason the tournament committee leader fought so hard in opposition to the use of allowances. It turns out Willie, the club's whiner-in-chief was a friend of Bud. Willie had Bud's ear and convinced him allowances just weren't fair and that he was being cheated. "Johnson's a four handicap and he's still playing as a four," Willie would whine. "I'm a twenty-two and I'm losing two full strokes to Johnson." His face would contort in wretched injustice. "Johnson's already eighteen strokes better than I am and now I'm losing two more. That's just not right!"

"Well, it's only a recommendation pal. We just won't use it." Bud was always good to his friends like that.

Let's acknowledge one more bit of grand larceny when playing team games. The instant a game is structured such that one or more balls do not count toward the team's score, you've opened the door to the "numerical manipulators", a.k.a., the sandbaggers. Once someone is out of the hole, bad things just seem to happen. Putts seem to run by the hole a little further. Some guys seem to practice their trick shots a little more often. In the words of our whiner-in-chief, "Never make a putt you don't need." But they still post the score!

After reviewing the data for about ten thousand rounds of golf, I found it interesting to discover that average gross scores for games where all balls counted were one to two strokes lower than for games where some balls didn't count. I'm sure it was just coincidence, once again, sort of like the oxygen molecules returning to the corner of the room. It can happen you know.

Before we leave the subject of managing the numbers, I offer one more bit of what I believe is unequivocal proof of how commonplace it has become. In the ideal world where the playing field is truly level, where everyone is honest and conscientious, the odds of a player winning a tournament with one hundred participants are roughly one-in-one-hundred. The computer program I use to analyze the data has a feature that predicts the chances a given team will win a tournament. In a particular Member/Member Tournament, fifty-one teams competed. The night prior to the tournament, the participants conducted their calcutta. Many tens of thousands of dollars were spent buying the teams. If someone would have purchased the top eight teams as predicted by the program, he would have spent a total of about twenty percent of the total value of the pot. He would have taken home nearly sixty-five percent of the total pot. The previous year, the return on "investment" would have been even higher.

So what's the point? Is it that the program does a good job? It's tough to argue with the results. But they beg the question, "How is the program so successful in picking the winners if the playing field is level?" The obvious answer is that the playing field isn't level. The program just uses algorithms to identify those individuals whose numbers are better managed than other golfers. If golfers weren't manipulating the numbers and the Handicap Committee was doing its job, the program would predict a fifty-one way tie for first place. The mere fact that people are bidding high amounts for some teams while other teams sell for a few quid pretty well proves that someone believes there are great inequities, a.k.a., cheaters in the field.

Seven – The Art of Missing Putts

"Never make a putt you don't need," Willie would always say. Although Willie got the credit for this statement at our club, I'm pretty confident he wasn't the first to say it. And he certainly won't be the last. I've played with Willie. It seems like he runs hot and cold. I've seen him when his putts would find the hole from all parts of the green. It was as if there was a giant sucking sound with a flag stick at the source. When I first joined the club, Willie asked me if I'd partner with him in a two man best ball tournament. We won (my last win at the club) and it was largely on the basis of his lights-out putting skills.

Maybe the batteries on his putter's GPS run down now and again. I've seen him putt as if he was aiming at a moving hole. He couldn't make a thing. Coincidentally, this seemed to happen when he was playing one of the weekly team games and his partner was already in for par or birdie. Willie's ball didn't count and it was a good thing because he would three-putt from ten feet. He just lost his feel. He never seemed to miss the two-footers. That would make him look suspicious. But a fifteen footer would somehow come up six feet short or run six feet past the hole. "They just aren't watering these greens the way they should," he'd complain. I felt sorry for the guy at least until the next tournament when his skills seemed to return.

Who hasn't left a fifteen foot putt six feet short? Or run a putt six feet past the hole? The pros do it from time-to-time. Of course we're going to do it. So there's no way you can get away with accusing someone of intentionally missing putts in order to pad his handicap. Or is there?

I'm coming back to the data. Remember Figure 6, the one showing the scoring probability on a given hole for any golfer? The bell curve – it has a peak at the most probable score and falls off gradually on either side of the peak as lower and higher scores become less probable. The scratch golfer's peak is close to par and the bogey golfer's peak is close to bogey. The important characteristic on these and nearly all scoring probability curves is that they are relatively smooth and gradual.

Now look at Figure 8. It is very real data from a very real golfer. It is not from Willie, but it just may be from one of his disciples. Note that his score probability distribution curve has a tumor on the right hand side. Rather than fall off smoothly like nearly every other curve examined, his actually increases at about one stroke over his average. Coincidentally, this is when he would normally be out of the hole in individual play or unnecessary in a two man team game. The curve is "unnatural" and indicates some manipulation is underway.

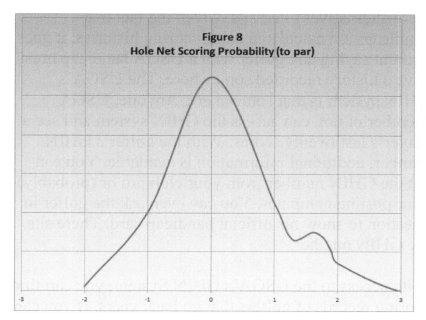

Figure 8
Hole Net Scoring Probability (to par)

It's true that you have to have a significant number of hole-by-hole scorecards to collect enough data to prove this type of manipulation. If you beat the bushes enough, you may discover it's possible to round up the records. Some clubs retain scorecards, especially from tournaments and weekly events, for a time. Some groups within clubs keep detailed records and may be willing to share them with you. In that the essence and spirit of the USGA Handicap System rests upon "peer review", you would certainly expect those who respect the game to be willing, if not anxious, to share whatever information they have available.

Let's assume that you are unable to get your hands on sufficient hole-by-hole data to prove your case. Are

there alternatives? Perhaps. Given the fact that
handicaps are calculated using scoring histories, it goes
without saying any golfer with a USGA handicap must
have a history recorded somewhere. The USGA's
GHIN system is that somewhere. Anyone, USGA
Member or not, can access the GHIN system and see a
player's last twenty scores. With the golfer's GHIN
number, additional information is available. You can
get the GHIN number from your club pro or (probably)
your posting computer. You can even ask the golfer in
question to show his official handicap card. There sits
the GHIN number.

With access to the USGA's GHIN System, you can find
scoring records of golfers that go back years. If you can
look at your old club newsletters or websites or
otherwise find out which dates involved individual play
versus team best ball play, you can review the average
scores for the suspect and see if best ball scores run
significantly higher than individual scores. It may be an
indicator that someone is sandbagging. Does it
conclusively prove someone's cheating? No, but it's
another piece of evidence. Not only that, it is
sufficiently time-consuming that it will give you
something to do on your rainy non-golf days when
there are no cartoons on TV.

There are a thousand and one other ways to "miss
putts" and run up your score. When you go to the range,
the goal is frequently to work on a particular aspect of

your game that needs to be strengthened. If you're in a best ball match and your partner is looking strong on the green, what better time to practice that nearly impossible flop-shot from a tight lie? Par five and your partner's eighty yards out in two? Give it a shot; I'll bet you can put the monster hook on your shot to get it around the big tree. You could be putting for eagle. Or maybe you'll be hitting a provisional ball hoping to save double-bogey. Handicap management comes in many different forms. You need to carry two-forty to get over the water. Wind's in your face. Partner's in good shape. What the hell – give it a go. (Don't use a new ball.) Oops – another double-bogey, but a gallant effort. And you're looking better for the next tournament.

Sometimes excessive risk taking on the golf course is nothing short of foolhardy. At other times, it is sly and strategically propitious.

Eight – The Myth of the Handicap Committee

It wasn't my idea. Somehow, Jim Horn found out that my mathematical background was a bit stronger than average. He started a campaign to have an additional seat added to the previously cloistered Handicap Committee. There had been grumblings about the Committee not being sufficiently proactive and Horn thought I might be able to take some steps to quell the epidemic of sandbagger's disease that had plagued the club. Not that our club was any worse than some other clubs, but there was no doubt that a little bit of handicap hygiene could go a long way toward bringing a healthier tournament environment. The powers that were saw no harm in adding a seat to the Committee and I agreed to serve and to do my best to do what was reasonable and right in the spirit of the USGA Handicap System. I only half-jokingly titled myself the Committee's "forensic statistician".

The first few meetings amounted to a grand awakening. Like a child in a forest, I had assumed the handicap world was pure, efficient and imbued with goodness and righteousness. I was shaken awake when I learned the Committee was composed of four individuals. The young club pro sat on the Committee as a non-voting member.

After the pro, the first member was the head of the Men's Golf Group, a guy who had an uncanny habit of winning the tournaments at the club, who knew arithmetic had something to do with "numbers", but wasn't sure how. To this day, he has neither read nor fully grasped the USGA Handicap System's manual. I've never seen him take the initiative on any handicap action and he generally laid low whenever anyone else did. The only time I've ever seen him take a stand on a Committee matter was when it involved a partner of his in an upcoming tournament and then he was generally strongly opposed to any action that would adversely impact his chances of winning.

The second member was the head of the Women's Golf Group. Frankly, she never said a word, didn't appear to have any interest or involvement and missed more meetings than she attended. To this day, I don't know if the lady has a speaking voice or merely served as a table decoration at those meetings which she did attend.

The third was the "Rules Nazi". This was a woman who insisted on being recognized as the world's foremost authority on the rules of golf even though her batting average on rule interpretation usually wasn't much higher than that of a utility infielder on a Class B ball club. Any time she weighed in on a subject (which was most of the time), she usually prefaced her comments with a recitation of her curriculum vitae and a litany of the various tournaments she had monitored or otherwise attended. When I later learned how important it was to her that people recognized her as having a vastly superior position in the golf world, I was somewhat surprised she didn't carry a small device that would play music leading to a voluminous crescendo as she approached the end of her list of accomplishments. It wasn't clear why she was on the Committee. She held no special position at the club, only a divine seat in the hallowed halls of her mind.

The fourth and (before my appointment) final position on the Committee was occupied by the Chairman. The consummate "nice guy", he was always smiling, friendly and helpful. However, by his own admission later on, he was a bit rusty on the rules and although he had for years held the position of chairman, he let the "Rules Nazi" run the show. She wanted to; he did not.

Now the Committee had a fifth, me – the forensic statistician. I watched in stunned amazement and thought, "What the hell have I gotten myself into?"

Over the next few months, I dutifully reviewed some of the club's miscreant suspects. I found some who seemed to have developed some form of writer's cramp (no doubt related to using putters with oversized grips) when it came time to record their correct scores in a timely manner. There were five handicap adjustments in one month just prior to a big tournament. I soon learned that this was not only a record for the Handicap

Committee, it was more than had been done collectively in the previous few years. For a fleeting period, I began to believe we were actually doing something worthwhile on behalf of the club membership.

Over time, we moved forward. But it became increasingly apparent that all was not transparent. The Rules Nazi, became president of the WGG and since the former WGG president had no reason to remain on the Handicap Committee, it was magically reduced by one seat. We were now four again.

Over time, we seemed to strike a marginally functional working relationship and actually accomplished a few things worthwhile. It wasn't always done without metaphorical bloodshed, but we were taking steps. I had learned to mouth the words of the Rules Nazi's resume whenever she was about to speak, sort of like pretending to sing the hymns in church while sitting in the back row. This later proved to be a strategic mistake on my part. I was inadvertently sowing the seeds of my own destruction. Little did I know it would lead to a coup d'état.

The Rules Nazi approached me one day and asked if I would be willing to become the Chairman of the Committee. I assumed she was joking and more or less ignored the question. A couple of weeks later, I was approached again and both she and her husband said they thought I could do a good job and that I should consider taking the position. I pointed out that we already had someone in the position and that I didn't think he had any intention of stepping down. "We'll just vote him out," she said with a matter-of-fact look on her face. I told her I would give it some thought.

I dutifully mulled over the idea. I reflected upon my previous year on the Committee and realized some improvement could definitely be made. There was little if any advance preparation for meetings. An "agenda" was an unheard of thing. The criteria for reviewing a golfer's performance seemed to involve little more than whether or not that golfer was liked by the Committee members. Friends were immune from review. Enemies were guilty until proven innocent and then still guilty. The satiation of egos took precedence over fairness and duty.

In other words, the first myth of the Handicap Committee was that it existed. If it was serving its purpose, it was a purpose that had no place in the USGA's Handicap System manual.

With the naiveté of a child, I convinced myself that if the Chairman's position were to become open, I would be willing to serve and would endeavor to do my best to make the Committee function in a manner that would be consistent with the mission of the USGA. There are words to describe this type of idealistic delusion; none of them are flattering. I told the Rules Nazi I would serve if it was deemed appropriate. I also insisted that the current Chairman be recognized for his long standing service and that if he was to give up his position it would be on his terms and with honor.

The new golfing season opened with me at the helm of a rudderless ship adrift on troubled seas. I attempted to create some organization and some review standards that hadn't existed previously. I had two primary goals. One was to take personalities out of the review equation. The second was to expand the Committee somewhat so that it was no longer a small cabal perceived as serving their own personal interests rather than the overall interests of the club's members.

The Committee grew to eight with the addition of three respected and mathematically competent club members. The review process was defined so that objective and defensible measures were used to identify golfers in need of "attention".

The most significant improvement in operation concerned the implementation of "blind reviews". The Committee chairman and the one individual presenting the data knew the identity of the subject under review. No one else on the Committee was aware of who was being scrutinized. Sometimes we went to great lengths to make sure no identifying information was revealed in the presentation of the data. Suddenly personalities were no longer a factor. Nothing but the actual data mattered.

Despite the immediate and rather obvious success of the program, the Rules Nazi steadfastly opposed the plan. She vehemently argued that she needed to know the identity of the person under review. She claimed she would be totally objective, but that somehow, the person's name was of critical importance. Others on the Committee could only wonder how she could justify her demands. Certain USGA officials also wondered why she insisted on knowing the names of the subjects.

It seemed like a good time for a test. I knew that the Rules Nazi had a deep hatred for one particular golfer at the club. She "knew" he was an unrelenting cheat, a reprobate that should have his handicap reduced pretty much because she said so. I took a complete set of this guy's data and "masked" it by altering play dates, scores, handicaps and winnings while still maintaining his pattern of play. It wasn't clear to whom I was referring. I then wrote a column on our blog asking for input from all the club members on what action the Handicap Committee should take with this golfer. I was so successful in disguising the identity of the golfer that even he didn't realize the article was about him.

The blog has a couple hundred regular subscribers and usually gets a couple hundred more readers straggling in. The title of the article was _You're Now in Charge of the Handicap Committee. A "Real" Review._

A significant number of members took the bait and submitted their suggestions either in the form of comments on the web site or off-line in private communications. No one thought the evidence was compelling enough to take immediate action. The most severe recommendation was to "continue to watch" the golfer.

About a month later, a meeting of the Handicap Committee found the Rules Nazi frothing. When the meeting convened and she had the floor, she launched a full assault on the handicap devil from hell. She found it all but impossible to keep her attack blind and the Committee soon knew the target of her vitriol. Although her evidence for a handicap reduction wasn't nearly as detailed as that presented in the blog article, in many respects, it did look similar. It shouldn't have been a surprise because the subject of the blog column was in fact the same person she now had in her crosshairs.

Before she knew his name, it was "Watch". Yet her attack was vigorous against the person whom she knew. Personalities undeniably had a profound impact on her decision making process. Without a name, there was nothing of great concern. With a name and a history of not liking the person, it was "Let's burn him at the stake!"

It should be clear by now that with most Handicap Committees, objectivity is a lofty goal, but a fleeting mirage. It is said that you should never piss off the cook because you'll never know what you'll be served. The same can be said for the Handicap Committee. Not a lot of them will go after their close friends. Fewer yet will act against their playing partners in upcoming events.

Speaking of acting against your friends and playing partners, the proof is in the darkness of the Committee meeting room. The head of the Men's Golf Group, the guy who warmed one of the seats in the Handicap Committee meeting room, had an extreme case of "perpetual serendipity". This is an affliction that results in a "trophular outbreak" and an ongoing need to clear additional shelf space in his trophy room. His tournament success would make Tiger Woods envious, but oxygen molecules . . . Oh, never mind.

When a completely blind review with overwhelming statistical evidence was presented to the Committee, there was unanimous agreement that something was amiss, even if it was just a very exceptional alignment of the stars. The odds of having a scoring pattern as presented were so incredibly small that no one in the room could accept them. There was discussion as to the appropriate course of action. When it had been settled and it came time for the formal vote, the identity of the person in question had been detected. It turned out to be the playing partner of the MGG president, the same one with whom he had partnered to win the previous year's Member/Member tournament and the President's Cup tournament and the national qualifier for a prestigious event. Suddenly, the prez decided that the statistics were not so overwhelming after all. He voted against censure of his partner.

His partner was "adjusted" anyway and coincidentally, they finished one stroke out of the money in the club's biggest tournament of the year. More than $50,000 was on the line.

A month later, the bandit who had been ruthlessly assaulted by the Rules Nazi was again before the Committee. The Members agreed on a continuation of a two stroke adjustment for the man. Mr. Prez again hemmed and hawed and resisted taking the action. He finally abstained from the vote. We soon learned the review was for his chosen partner in an upcoming qualifier for a national event.

Once again the myth of the Handicap Committee's existence was shrouded in darkness and came into question. I had believed we existed. After all, we did come together to meet at some location. We talked about handicap related issues. But we didn't always seem to be there when it came time to do our jobs.

The conclusion to be drawn from these (and countless other untold stories) is that despite the nominal existence of the Committee, only the most gullible truly believe it always acts objectively and in the best interests of everyone concerned.

Moral of the story . . . Buddy up to anyone on the Committee. Always smile at them. Tell them their shots are great on the course. Let them know you envy their talents, skills and ongoing good fortune. Buy them a toddy from time-to-time. Above all else, say, "Wow! Impressive resume you've got there. We're sure lucky to have you around."

In many cases, the reality is that if the Committee didn't exist, it might be an improvement to the club.

Nine – Now What?

Cheating in golf is as old as the game itself. In the previous pages, you've learned how some people game the system. You've also learned some of the ways you can identify them and take steps to stop the practice. You've got some tools that you can use for good or for evil. Frankly, evil is more profitable, but there's always that problem of looking the man in the mirror directly in the eyes. Your call.

There are some tournaments where the competition truly isn't about golf as much as it is about which bandit can escape with all of the other bandit's money. If you're not a bandit, cheat, crook, thief or other life form known to inhabit the murkier areas of muskrat infested water hazards, you have no business entering these tournaments unless you're just contributing to a good cause (like the winner's budget for beer). Handicapped tournaments open to the public at large draw players from the recesses of the golf world's sewers. Throw in a calcutta (an auction of the teams prior to the tournament where the proceeds are returned to the participants as prize money) and you might as well empty all of the prisons and give the inmates golf clubs, guns, whiskey and your wife. You're nothing but the victim.

Member/Guest tournaments are generally viewed as "fun" events. Despite the best efforts of the tournament committee, the task of verifying handicaps for the guests is all but impossible. The club staff's principal goal is that everyone has fun. This translates into "Don't rock the boat." It's not going to be fun nor will it foster great human relations by penalizing a member's guest before he sets foot on the first tee. The Handicap Committee could undertake the job, but as you now know, the Handicap Committee may have other functions that don't necessarily include promoting equitable competition. In the Member/Guest, one of the members is bringing in a ringer. Unless that person is you, you'd better come to grips with the reality that you may have a wonderful time, but you probably don't have to worry about writing your heart-felt acceptance speech and clinging to the memories of your victory. Have fun.

If your goal in selecting a tournament is to enjoy yourself and winning isn't part and parcel to that goal, any tournament will fill the bill. If it means a chance to play with someone you've always wanted to meet, give it a shot. If it means seeing a course you've always wanted to see, go for it. But if having a realistic chance at a victory is even a secondary goal, consider staying home. Let's assume you're an absolutely honest golfer and that you faithfully post every score. Let's really take it to the next level and assume everyone in your club does the same. You're as close to the ideal and level playing field as one could ever hope to get. There are still considerations that may help give you a slight edge.

If the results are solely based upon individual play, gross or net, it becomes simple. Shoot some good golf. Chide your Handicap Committee into doing its job fairly and objectively. In other words, eliminate the fudging, cheating and banditry.

If team play is an issue, you've got some decisions to make. Does the club or tournament committee properly apply handicap allowances? If you're a fairly steady golfer, pair up with a golfer with a higher handicap. Take advantage of the extended probability curve. If you're a high handicapper, find a partner known for his consistency, even if his handicap is in the same range as yours.

Handicaps fluctuate over time. In the Arizona desert, for example, handicaps tend to swing an average of about three strokes over the course of a year. Over-seeding in the early fall means scores soar as the transition from summer to winter grass makes the courses play tougher. Handicaps fall from late spring through the summer as the courses dry out and 240 yard drives roll out to 270 yards. In areas where winter causes courses to close, handicaps tend to rise in the spring with rust on the swing and frost on the ground. If you're picking a partner for your member/guest tournament, favor the one whose handicap has peaked given the area in which he normally plays. Many factors come into play when selecting your partner for a team based tournament. Handicap is the biggest one. Is it an honest one? Is it "timed" right?

The overriding message I've tried to present in this book is that golf is a stochastic process. That means that it follows the laws of statistics. When a golfer consistently performs where his numbers are well outside the range predicted by the laws of statistics, there's a villain in the house. Golfers shoot their handicaps between twenty and twenty-five percent of the time. If a guy is consistently above fifty percent, you're the sucker – not him. If his away score differentials differ by more than a few strokes from his home score differentials, you're being cheated.

If you've picked up this book to get some tips on how to win, you can either use the information presented to catch the crooks or you can use it to join them. Let your conscience be your guide. However, if you continue ignoring the problems, if your Handicap Committee remains unaccountable and largely invisible, if you keep giving yourself two foot putts, you'd better set your sights on enjoying the tournament rather than winning it. Chances are you've spotted the guy accepting the trophy a couple of extra strokes.

"I told you that son of a bitch was going to win. He's the biggest sandbagger in the club."

About the Author

h. Alton Jones is a native of Detroit, Michigan. He is a "High Honors" graduate of Michigan State University where he attended undergraduate and graduate school in chemical engineering. He studied for his Ph.D. at the University of Arizona in Tucson. He began his writing and reporting career in Ann Arbor, Michigan in 1966 and worked in the broadcast news industry in Detroit, Denver, Miami and Portland, Oregon. After leaving the news business to found and operate a successful software company, he returned to the media world in 2000 writing a regular column in an Arizona newspaper for nearly ten years. He is the author of the book *The Man on the Bench*. Together with his wife of thirty years, Liz McCarty, he still travels the world seeking adventure and new horizons. When not travelling, he plays golf in Scottsdale, Arizona.

www.HowToCheatInGolf.com

Other Books by h. Alton Jones
  The Man on the Bench (www.TheManOnTheBench.com)
  Widow's Peak (with Liz McCarty)

CPSIA information can be obtained at www.ICGtesting.com
Printed in the USA
LVOW01s2236110814

398675LV00010B/14/P